The Exceptional Small Business Owner

Building a Reputation That Will Bring Employees
and Customers Flocking To Your Door
(Hint: It's All About You!)

Arlene Doeden

Dedication

This book is dedicated to entrepreneurs everywhere, who truly dance to a different beat. Thank you for dreaming your dreams, building foundations under those dreams, and then having the tenacity to see those dreams unfold. You are a courageous bunch, and without you, countries around the world would be at an economic loss. Keep the fires burning. The world needs you!

With Much Gratitude To:

My husband, Ray, who carried our household so I could write this book. I'm sure at times it wasn't easy working all those truck driving hours while I sat on our porch with a pot of tea, typing away.

All the caregivers who worked for me. Your input was so much appreciated. I learned a lot from you and loved working with each of you!

The now out-of-print book I read many years ago, *Management: A Biblical Approach*. The main theme of the book was this: the higher you rise in a company or organization, the more of a servant you will become to those under you. It became the basis of my management style.

Christine Grace Magnussen, my good friend who constantly encouraged me, even when I was doing my most vigorous foot dragging.

Table of Contents

Preface

Welcome to *The Exceptional Small Business Owner: Building A Reputation That Will Bring Employees And Customers Flocking To Your Door (Hint, it's All About You!)*

This small book has been a long time coming. It was conceived about 14 years ago, even before I started my first business. A friend encouraged me to start my own business and then write a book about it. I jotted that down on the *mythical 3X5 card* and filed it in the back of my brain. But actually, it wasn't too long after that conversation that I started my first business, which happened to be a Tea Room.

The learning curve was high, and I wondered what I had gotten myself into. I was driven by passion and a fierce determination to make it work. I read everything I could get my hands on regarding business, employees, merchandising, marketing, food service, and of course, teas.

I went to tea conferences, and learned to bake great scones and wonderful soups made from scratch, all under the watchful eye of a hovering Health Department. I did really well at some things, and was horrible at others. I even attempted a partnership, but that is another book. Alas, I had broken too many rules of business and closed after three years.

I felt like a failure and absolutely did not think I was ready to write a book on it. But then I started two Adult Family Homes. The lessons learned during my Tea Room venture prepared me for my Adult Family Home business. I had many caregivers who worked for me and I received many compliments about my management style.

Caregivers who had moved on to other jobs would relay horror stories to me about their current job and thanked me for being a great boss. One told me she was glad to have worked for me first, giving her the confidence she needed. One caregiver told me I should write a book.

Ding ding ding! Did she really say that?

You might think my arm is cramping from patting myself on the back, but really, I was hearing this over and over from many people who were involved in the Adult Family Home business. I honestly did not see what I was doing that was different than anyone else.

Caring for up to six elderly people with various kinds and stages of dementia in my home was not only an honor, but very rewarding. It also can be mentally fatiguing. After seven years of caring for a total of 24 residents, I decided to retire. I retrieved that old tattered 3x5 card from the back of my brain and determined that now is the right time to pen that book.

Introduction

This book was written primarily from my own personal experience of what worked well for me. There are a gazillion (I love this word and use it a lot) books out there on management, leadership, and business. I have read many of them, and found that much of the information contained in them are concepts I had already employed.

All to say, that I have not just regurgitated information in these pages gleaned from every other book on the market. What I have written is a combination of ideas and processes from many resources including books, help from family members, friends, bookkeepers, accountants, seminars and conferences, past and current experience, employees, and plain old trial and error.

I had several readers in mind when I wrote this book. They are the following:

Managers

Managers are often given the autonomy to develop their own style. Working directly with staff, they hold a key role in the business environment.

Those Dreaming of, or Planning to, Start Their Own Business

There are a gazillion puzzle pieces to put together when starting a new business. Deciding early on what your business model is going to look like, what your management style is, your perceptions of customer service and even your view of the world will all impact the success of your future business. Contemplating and deciding on what kind of owner/manager you want to be will give you a huge head start on developing your business. I hope the stories and topics in this book will help you get the mental wheels turning on the more subtle aspects of owning your own business.

Small Business Owners in Their First to Third Years of Operation

Sometimes we get locked into doing and thinking the same things, even when they are no longer productive, simply because that is how we have always done things. My hope is that this book will be like an extra pair of eyes, allowing you to see new ways to think and do. Those who are open to change, and are willing to "try on" new ways to think and do, will likely experience the greatest success.

The "DUH" factor

Some of what I have written here might seem elementary. So much so that you might think that if a person is breathing they probably know this stuff. Not always so. Entrepreneurs come from all walks of life with varied educational backgrounds and perceptions of the business world, depending on what they have been taught, told, or experienced.

I not only write to the more savvy business minded, but also to the dreamer who has little background in business, but has been bitten by the entrepreneurial bug. We've all been there at one time.

As A Last Note

I use the words *owner* and *manager* interchangeably. New business owners often ARE the managers in the early days of a business. If your business has progressed to the point where you have hired a manager, you can apply the content to both you, the business owner, and your manager.

Disclaimer

I do not guarantee any of the information in this book will work for you. What I do know is that it has worked for me and countless other business owners. Each of us brings our own personality and business style to the business mix. You may look at the information here as guidelines if you wish.

CHAPTER 1

Integrity

Who Are You, Really?

Being a great business owner starts with operating from a great set of principles. What do you believe in? Is life black and white with a little bit of gray? Or a lot of gray? On what do you base your daily decisions?

A radio host I used to listen to always ended her show by saying, "Now go and do the right thing." What is that? Sometimes doing the right thing isn't always easy to know; much less do. Nevertheless, everyone must define for themselves what principles they will operate from.

Who or what defines your concepts of right and wrong? What does your moral compass say? Do you want to see how close you can come to the legal line without crossing it, or stay as far away from the line as you can get? (Jail time and/or fines are never attractive business options).

These are not rhetorical questions. They will determine virtually every aspect of your business life including:

- How you relate to your staff, customers, and venders

- How you handle your financial affairs

- What you do with your time

- How you operate legally

- Your day-to-day operations

- Your marketing strategy

- Your communication style

Many people will try to compartmentalize their lives, believing that what they do in their personal life has no bearing on their job. I don't see it that way. If you feel justified in yelling profanities at your spouse, it will most likely "leak over" into the job by yelling at employees, especially in times of stress. If you are a bitter, negative person with a pessimistic world view, that also will leak over. By the same token, if you are fair, self-controlled, friendly and kind, that will also leak over to the job. Believe me, the "real self" will eventually show up in attitude, words, or deeds.

I Give You My Word!

How many times have you said this to family and friends throughout your life? Our word is absolutely everything. In the workplace it will build trust and loyalty among your staff, customers, and venders.

If you say yes, then follow through. If you say no, then follow through. If you cannot follow through due to circumstances beyond your control, then say so and work on a solution.

For example, if you told one of your departments that you were going to order five reams of paper tomorrow, then make sure the paper is ordered. There might be three employees who can't do their job if you don't do yours. If you announce that you will call someone, take care of a problem, look up information, or pick up supplies, then make sure you carry out those tasks in a timely manner. Showing up at 4:00 PM with supplies that had a 2:00 PM shipping deadline does not work.

Many owners have the attitude that because they are the boss, they can do things in their own time frame or when the mood strikes them. It won't take long for your staff (and customers) to realize they have been "blown off." But worse yet, they will no longer trust you. Without trust, they will no longer respect you. It's been said that people don't leave bad companies, they leave bad bosses. Enough said.

YOU Setting The Bar

Setting the bar for high standards is a top-down process. If the owner does not care, he/she cannot expect employees to care. When I worked for a private ambulance company, my supervisor (also one of the owners of the company) was a real stickler for detail. If reports were not written correctly, you kept getting it put in your box to rewrite until it was correct. Our ambulance response calls were critiqued as well. Most all of my crew members appreciated the high standard we were being held to, but there were always a few who felt more comfortable taking the low road.

But really, who would you rather work for? Someone who did not give a rip about quality of product or service? Or someone who actually believed in and cared about their mission, work, staff, customers and their business? When you are the owner, YOU get to set the bar not only for yourself and your company but for your staff as well.

Set the bar high.

CHAPTER 2

Professionalism

Be a Drama-Free Work Place

Believe it or not, I will be talking about business owners here as well as paid managers. Owners are people too. We have unfortunate things happen to us like everyone else. The dog got out and it took an hour to get him back; you slammed your thumb in the car door; or you might be dealing with more serious issues like a volatile relationship, or trying to find care for aging parents.

The frustrations or pain from what is going on in the personal life can create drama in the workplace. The manager can "dump" his woes on his staff which creates drama. As hard as it is, managers must leave their troubles at the door. Your staff looks up to you for leadership and the ability to get a job done.

That's not to say you can't be human, but there is a huge difference between coming in and telling your staff you had a rough morning, as opposed to ranting to them about the rip-roaring, blow-by-blow description of the verbal argument you had with your spouse that morning. If you find yourself in an emotional place where you don't think you can function, or even just give others your best, delegate your day's assignments and take the day off. I've been there.

My Story

My story is about a time when I was too emotionally distraught to do my job and needed to step down to allow myself some recovery time. It was in my 5th year as an EMT working for a volunteer fire department. This was before I had started my businesses.

I had gone to a weekend-long emergency medical services training conference that was being held in my town. The last conference workshop was held on a Sunday afternoon and was presented by one of the agencies that coordinated rescue and recovery operations at the 1995 Murrah Building bombing site in Oklahoma City.

Training videos were graphic and training was intense—as it needed to be for our local firefighters to be prepared in the event of a like mass causality incident in our area. By the end of the conference, there was not a dry eye in the room. Now here was my problem. I was scheduled that night to teach a group of small children at my church. Trying to maintain the tough firefighter, I-can-deal-with-anything image,

I drove to church to carry out my assignment, even though I was experiencing uncontrollable sobbing.

When I got to church, I put on my painted smile for the kids, but their happy excited energy only brought back my uncontrollable sobbing. I actually had to pull another teacher in to cover my class as it was evident I should not have even come.

If you are dealing with emotional trauma, it's okay to take a day off. Or two. Your business will survive without you. Take care of the few things that can ONLY be done by you and ONLY if absolutely necessary and delegate absolutely EVERYTHING else. You owe your staff and customers your best, both physically and mentally; not to mention recovery time for yourself.

What Kind Of A Duck Are You, Anyway?

There is an old saying that says if you look like a duck, walk like a duck, and talk like a duck, you must be a duck. So what kind of duck are you? When you are the owner of a company, you want everything about you to scream, "I am a Professional!" Let's start with what you look like.

What do your staff and customers see when they first walk up to you? There have been volumes written about first impressions. Let's start with your clothes.

Clothes

Styles vary from region to region, by age groups, by company policies as well as personal tastes. How do you want to appear to your customers? Casual? Very White collar? Keep in mind I am not talking about when you are at home lounging, but at work. No matter what you choose, there are some absolutes that fall into the realm of "professional" in about 98% of most businesses.

- For women, keep cleavage to a minimum. This includes when you are standing up AND bending over. Note that I am not advocating 18th century button-up-the-neck, no-skin-showing clothing. Modest and tasteful are words that come to mind. It is very possible to maintain femininity without looking like an advertisement for a local red light district.

- For men AND women, no posterior cleavage. Low rider pants are very fashionable but bending over often reveals the proverbial *plumber's crack* that most people do not equate with professionalism. If low-rider pants are worn, make sure the shirt or blouse is long enough to cover any indiscreetness.

- Torn, ripped, or frayed jeans would be better on your non-work days if those are your style. Again, your work clothes should set you apart as the owner/manager. The desire that you may have to connect with your customers, can cause the line to blur between casual and sloppy. A skateboard shop owner still would benefit from wearing a pair of kakis and a tee shirt rather than ripped jeans and a shirt that has the sleeves hacked off. It all boils down to the message you want to convey to your customers. Do you want to present as, "Hey, I'm one of you," or "I am the owner, an authority on my product or service, and I am here to serve you"? Your knowledge and expertise will speak for itself when it comes to connecting with your customers, conveying that you are like minded.

- Tattoos and body piercing are forms of art and beauty enhancement. Overdone—even if you own those types of establishments—can make you look like the in-your-face, new kid on the block wanting to make friends, rather than an expert in your field.

Note, I did not say tattoos need to be covered, and piercings need to come out. What I am saying is if there is not much of your skin that is NOT tattooed or you have 20 piercings in your face, or no one can understand you because of your tongue piercing, you might want to rethink the message you are sending your customers. Having said that, there are still some industries where tattoos or body piercings are not tolerated. The health care industry is one and will probably remain so.

Again, you want to set yourself apart as the owner and expert. To illustrate my point, when was the last time you walked into a classy jewelry store, to have the owner come out to assist you with 6 rings on each finger and 10 necklaces draped around his or her neck?

- Grooming is a biggie. Does your shirt look like it has been living in a laundry basket for the past week? Shoelaces tied? Teeth brushed? Socks match? Your hair actually looks like you spent some time on it? Pants zipped? These all go back to the "duh" factor, but in the busy-ness of life, and trying to get out the door in the morning, some of these things can be overlooked. You are not only dressing for your customers, but setting the bar for your staff.

- And then there are the words that flow from the mouth. The tongue can be a difficult thing to tame. I have had encounters with managers who looked like they just stepped out of a band box but once they open their mouth, all their credibility disappears. The following highlights some areas you will want to be mindful of.

- No potty mouth. Can't think of a better way to say it? Swearing today has become so accepted, that you become exceptional just by NOT swearing. Many believe that you raise children to believe swearing is wrong and in fact chastise them for uttering the forbidden "damn" or "hell" they hear in school, or from their parents. After all, swearing is only okay for grownups, right? I remember my Mom telling me when I was a late teen, that people who are educated and "polished" do not have a need to use explicative language to punctuate every sentence or thought. Good advice.

- Don't correct a staff member in front of others. This falls under the category of the T.E.A.M approach. That is the acronym for *Treat Everyone As Me*. No one likes to be embarrassed in front of others. Take the staff member aside to discuss the issue in private.

- No Gossip. This includes telling horror stories about employees both past and present. This includes verbally repeating mistakes any staff member may have made.

Lessons are usually learned when mistakes happen and often provide a new way to do or not do a task. It is certainly advantageous to provide rationale for your policies and procedures while training staff, but it is not necessary to reveal who screwed up, and how badly, that caused you to develop the current policy.

Gossip usually has a negative purpose that thrives in a factual void. Your business will fail if gossip is allowed to flourish.

- How you act is the last piece that will define you as the person in charge. The number one element I see is how well you handle stress. Owning and/or managing a small business is usually very stressful and frustrations can easily push you over the edge.

- Anger management is vital in your role as manager. I have seen owners pick up large items and throw them across the room in fits of rage. This obviously does not instill much confidence in your ability to function as a leader, especially by those who get to see and hear such lack of personal control. Work on changing the situations that frustrate you, and explore ways to deal with the situations you can't change.

- Striving to be fair will go a long way with your staff. Showing any kind of favoritism amongst your staff will be greeted with scorn towards you. I'm talking about the obvious kind of favoritism like hiring your unqualified best buddy over a currently experienced employee, or granting special days off, or overlooking tardiness of one particular employee that would not fly with other employees of the same position. There are times when you have to make some hard choices when choosing who to promote or who to let go. While you want to be as fair as possible, ultimately, you will want to do what is best for your business.

My Story

There was an occasion when I had to downsize by one employee in my adult family home. This meant I had to choose between two of my day staff members—who was going to go and who was going to stay. Tina had been there the longest, but had a hard time grasping many concepts between *clean and dirty,* which is essential in the healthcare field.

She had a tendency to be a little rougher with residents in our home, was not well liked by some of the residents' families. There were issues of trust I had with her as well.

Sally, on the other hand, had only worked for me for about eight months but was off the chart quality on every level. So, how did I make my decision? Since I was not a union shop, which uses seniority as the basis for such decisions, I chose quality of work as my base.

Tina perceived this as unfair, having worked there the longest; but ultimately, I (and you will too) needed to base my decision on what was best for my residents and my business. I did not retain Sally because I liked her the best, but simply because she WAS the best.

- Being fair to your staff while working out issues with a customer is also important. While I believe customers should be treated like royalty, that does not mean you should throw your staff under the bus while doing so. Your staff members are your greatest asset and you will be held with the highest regard when you stand by them.

Look for *what* is right, not *who* is right. Bend a rule in the customer's favor only if it will not minimize your employee. I would not allow any customer to browbeat, or verbally abuse any staff member, even if the customer was totally in the right. Giving your staff clear guidelines on your customer service polices will empower them and reduce customer conflicts. There really are some customers out there that you just don't want.

- Being fair to your customers is paramount if you want to retain them. That includes fair pricing, fair product or service, and fair customer service. You hear all the time that life isn't fair, but that does not apply in the business world. If customers feel you are gouging them, they will go elsewhere. If you deliver poor product or service, kiss your customer goodbye. If they receive their product Friday when you promised it the previous Monday, you won't be looking very good. If you mess up, make it right, whatever it takes.

My Story

My story has to do with when I was a no-show for an appointment with a coaching client. I totally spaced the appointment. I was moving my residence that week and was trudging through a bad case of bronchitis as well. I thought I had rescheduled the appointment, but had not. It was five days later that I realized I had stood up this client.

When I called her, she was very understanding and just wondered what had happened to me. Nevertheless, when I showed up for our next session, I brought the largest hanging basket of flowers I could find, as well as a coupon for a free extra session, over and above the one I had missed.

CHAPTER 3

Attitudes

Me Boss, You Slave

Unfortunately, the mentality of much of corporate America runs along the lines of "Me boss, you slave" attitude. That attitude is rarely verbally stated, but manifests itself in a hundred different ways. One might argue that a manager's role is to make sure tasks get done. That's certainly true, but too often is done with whip cracking rather than through leadership. Here are some samplings of the me-boss-you-slave manifestations.

- Leaving personal work space cluttered, expecting someone else to clean up after you is just as common in the small business world as in the corporate setting.

Many small business owners need to work shifts in the early years of their business. How do you leave that work space when your shift is over? Do you clean the area the same as you would expect your employees to do? Do you restock supplies so it is ready for the next shift? Do you pass down information or relate things that have come up on your shift?

My Story

My story involves just such a manager that I had a conversation with. Some of my part-time employees also worked for another home business like mine. I knew the owner and we had talked many times about many different issues. My staff had told me how frustrated they were, when they went to work there because they often had to clean up a whole sink full of dishes, including pots and pans, all from the owner and his family. This needed to be done before they could start their own busy morning of chores.

The owner had a typical me-boss-you-slave answer for this. "I pay this employee X amount of money anyway, so what's the difference?"

My answer? The difference is the message that is sent to the employee. That message is, "Because I am the owner, I do not have to be personally responsible for myself or the messes I make. After all, that is why I have employees."

If my family made any kind of meal, even just toast, we left the area like we were never there. It was assumed my staff were responsible for the residents we cared for. That is what they were hired for. Their job description did not include personal maid service for me and my family. Staff members who are treated like valued employees, instead of personal maids, will stick around longer, feel appreciated, and respect the owner more.

- Asking your employees to do tasks that are clearly your responsibility will cause resentment. This is especially true if the sole purpose is just because you don't want to do the task. This can be making phone calls that you don't want to make, filling out paperwork you find tedious, or giving a whole new area of responsibility to a staff member that you just don't think you have the time for. This manager's thinking is, "Hey, they are willing to do it, and it will lighten my load." The staff member is thinking, "Why is he asking me to do HIS job?

Tolerance—a Different Perspective

You hear a lot about tolerance these days. You hear it on radio, television and in print. There are political and religious groups that are formed around being tolerant. It is the word of the day. I'm here to tell you, that in the business world, it really is important.

My Story

This story is about a day back in 1989 when I visited a coffee shop while checking out the town of Bellingham, Washington. My family was planning to move here so I flew up to check out every aspect of Bellingham.

There was a very unique coffee shop that everyone told me I must go try out that was in "Old Town." The building was a 100-year-old brick building with an interior of wide plank flooring that creaked as you walked across it. The centerpiece in the room was a huge pot-bellied stove with tables and chairs positioned around it.

Coming from the Los Angeles area, this was quite unique for me, but not in a good way since I was a bit "uppity" at the time. I felt I had been transported back to the turn of the century (the last one, not the current one!). I was relieved to know that Bellingham had at least moved up to the 1960's when I saw customers coming in wearing bell bottom pants.

As I sat sipping my most delicious cup of espresso, I started to see men in business suits coming in, grabbing a quick cup to go. Women in business suits, high heels clicking across the wood floor, came bringing in their to-go mugs to be filled for the morning. Old men were sitting in corners, reading the paper that had been left by others as they sipped their coffee.

Two guys with hair in dreadlocks came in. Two moms, dressed just like me, came in with their children.

I was amazed how diverse their customer base was. This was not the only coffee shop in the area, but apparently they were the best. No signs were posted outside defining their perfect customer. Or how they needed to be dressed (except for the usual health department rules of shirts and shoes). Or what their personal belief system needed to be. People are people.

The guys with the dreadlock hair sought a place to visit while consuming a great beverage. The elderly man wanted a place to read the paper while drinking a great cup of coffee. The moms were enjoying a great breakfast with their children, while the business customers were able to take their cup of joe with them to enjoy during their early morning work hours. Everyone seemed happy.

Tolerance for various belief systems is something I had to deal with in my own business. I will tell you up front, that I have a very strong Christian belief system. I am also a "dyed in the wool" capitalist. I also believe that I don't have to buy into other people's belief systems in order to love and serve them. I can "meet" them wherever they are at in life. I had residents in my adult family home who were practicing Mormons, Jehovah's Witnesses, Seventh Day Adventists, Catholics, Christians, and many who professed to no religion at all. Some were Democrats and some were Republicans, and some were not interested in politics at all. I had staff that were professed atheists and some were Christian. Some staff had strong political views and some were still trying to figure it all out.

My viewpoint is that part of being professional, is recognizing that I am not the only one on the planet, even if I do think I am right. Again, people are people. Seeing the decline of a mom or dad due to dementia is painful and sad, regardless of religious persuasion. Democrats, Republicans, Independents, and those who could care less about the political scene, all want the best care for a declining loved one, as well as support for themselves. And here, providing the best product and service for my customers is where I want my focus (and yours) to be.

CHAPTER 4

Attributes

Be a Master Communicator

There are so many ways to give and receive information I am amazed we can communicate with each other at all. Just take a look below, at all of the ways we receive and interpret information.

- The words we use

- The emphasis we put on different words we use

- Body Language

- Voice inflection and volume

- Prior experiences (baggage) we bring with us in interpreting meaning of a conversation

Now add the non-face-to-face communication of texting, e-mail, Facebook, Twitter and other social media venues. And lastly, add in what our life experiences bring to a conversation.

Someone who is unsure of himself may well take a statement an entirely different way than someone who is confident. An employee who has had a prior bad experience with the Owner/manager, either real or perceived, can easily enter into a new conversation with a preconceived notion before a word is uttered.

Owners/managers can fall into the same trap working with difficult and demanding clients, vendors, or government agencies that may oversee their business.

Communication is key to how everything flows. It is the glue that gets jobs done. Good communication instills confidence and keeps everyone on the same page.

Communication with Your Staff

Initial Interview

It starts on day one. Well, even before day one, because it starts at the interview. *Time is money* usually means wasted time equals lost money. That is not the case with interviewing time. Long lengthy interviews are often thought of as unnecessary. I see the cost of brief, fill-the-shift-fast interviews very costly in the long run.

New hires have a higher learning curve and a shorter stay due to lack of information up front. I often cleared my calendar on interview days, spending at least thirty minutes, and sometimes longer, on applicants who exhibited strong possibilities. This is not only a time to see if I would want this applicant to work for me, but also if my work place would be a good fit for the applicant.

They may decide that they don't want to work at your place. Maybe after hearing the expectations, they would not be comfortable working for you. Unless I relay my expectations, they will not know dress codes, job duties, customer service policies, chain of command, safety procedures, their boundaries in decision making, as well as my personal business philosophy. If an applicant cannot buy into my business philosophy, or any of the other above mentioned policies, it is unlikely they will be a good fit. This is the best place to find that out.

Staff Meeting

Another communication tool is staff meetings. Unless they are paid, it is often hard to motivate everyone to come, especially for those who are not working on the day or time of the scheduled staff meeting. Even if paid, scheduling can still be a problem if the business operates twenty-four hours a day.

If staff meetings work well for you, keep the meetings to one hour with a written agenda. Have copies of the agenda for all staff to have in hand, if possible. This helps staff feel like they are part of a problem-solving team, rather than sitting in a classroom with a teacher at the helm.

This is a time to state what is going well, and what isn't. To give recognition, to discuss problems, and ask for input. There should be time allowed where staff can ask questions or clarify situations or policies. Time can get away fast, so the manager must also become a master facilitator keeping everyone on track. Honor everyone's time by starting and ending on time. Set up brief individual sessions with staff who feel they need more clarification, or have further questions or suggestions they would like to discuss.

How often you require staff meetings will be dependent on the amount of information to be discussed, the size of your staff, what changes are currently going on in your business, and of course, how well you facilitate. Staff meetings held monthly is usually considered the minimum. Some small businesses have a simple ten minute verbal pass-down time between shifts every day.

Communication Book

Yet another way to communicate with staff is through a *communication book*. It is a top down approach where the manager conveys information to his or her staff. It is required reading for each staff when coming on shift.

Once read, staff initials to ensure they have read the communication. This can be a communication book where managers update staff on policy changes, orders coming in or out; customer service issues; current status of equipment, products, or services; or a gazillion other need-to-know issues.

Since staff are reading this upon their arrival, and most likely relieving another staff member, it is best to keep communications brief and to the point. At the end of each day, it is important that the manager check the book to make sure everyone has initialed. A spiral bound notebook, or three ring binder works best. Staff who have been gone a few days can refer back to the days they were off. Once filled, file these notebooks away. They can be useful tools to refer back to if there is a discrepancy among staff regarding who knew what and when.

Communication books can also be for all employees to communicate with each other, to convey to their coworkers that are coming on shift what changes happened during the day, supplies that are getting low, or chores that did or did not get done.

This type of book comes with a word of warning. It can become a stab-in-the-back, snarling in-print cat fight. You know the communication book has declined to this level when you see entries that are just dripping with rage or sarcasm. Like lots of sentence underlining, a gazillion exclamation points!!!!!, VERY LARGE PRINT, not to mention the harsh words.

When a staff communication book is introduced as a communication tool, it's important to convey the purpose of it, both verbally and written. The objective is to pass on information that will help other employees know the status of the workplace when they arrive. It is not a place to vent personal feelings or "whip" their coworkers.

My experience has been that the largest point of contention in this type of communication book is feelings of others not carrying their weight by consistently leaving chores or part of their job undone, passing the extra work load on to the next shift. All staff need to know that they will have busy days and there will be times that not everything can be completed. If there seems to be a pattern of one individual having problems of completing work, or anything else for that matter, then that needs to be brought to the attention of the manager privately. Employees often don't see the bigger picture. They may not know that "Susan" also has to inventory six shelves of merchandise on her shift on Tuesdays. Maybe there really is a need to revamp the chore schedule. If this is the case, it would be an excellent agenda item for your next staff meeting. Ask for input. You would be amazed at the ingenuity of your staff.

There are fancy (and expensive) staff log software programs that you can buy where everyone types in their entry. There are also websites where you can download free templates for a staff log book, or at least get an idea on setting up a log book page. Then there is the old fashioned way of just getting a spiral or three ring binder and a stack of paper. Write the date across the top with a place for entries. Use whatever works best for your business. The goal is to keep information flowing.

Communication with your Customers

Good communication is also important with your customers:

- When taking orders

- Return policies

- Hours of operation

- Details about your products or services

- Delivery dates

When your customer leaves your store, whether it be brick and mortar or an online store, customers want to be crystal clear on what to expect when purchasing from you. It's the owner's job to ensure every detail of information they need or want (within reason) has been provided for them. If they have questions, answer them. If you don't know the answer, tell them you don't (honesty goes a long way with customers), but you will find out. Then do it. Get back with them on that information in a timely manner.

My Story

I had ordered a book from an online distributor, and since I am always looking for the latest information, I wanted to order the 3rd edition of an older book I already owned. The online information about the book said nothing about which edition it was. I purchased it anyway, hoping that it would be the edition I was wanting. It was not. Lesson learned.

My feedback to that seller was "instructive." It would have been nice if the seller had included which edition he was selling, keeping his customer in the forefront as opposed to his bottom line. I was foolish to purchase an item for which I did not have all the information. Next time, I will pass by a product or service if the information is skimpy. The best businesses not only want to sell their products and services, but also collect happy customers along the way.

Be Flexible

In a perfect world, supplies always come when promised, employees never get sick and the *in-box* on your desk never gets full. It is not likely we will ever live in that world. The dictionary defines flexible as "capable of being bent without breaking." Flexibility is a learned skill; easier for some, than for others.

I have worked with people who could not endure even the slightest change in task or schedule without falling apart. Being able to adapt to a changing work environment is critical for a manger. There most likely will be at least one staff, customer, or business operational *fire* you will need to put out every day. This is true even in the best run business. Learning to "think on your feet" is critical.

I found the most effective way to think on your feet, is to focus on possible solutions rather than what isn't working out right. Our first instinct is to go into panic mode. This is okay for about the first thirty seconds. Then you must move on to what your options are to fix the problem. After awhile, you don't even go through the panic stage. Focusing on options and choosing a solution becomes automatic No more than just a little speed bump in your day.

Be Organized

Running a business can get crazy! It is imperative that you are organized. If you are a small business owner, you are likely to have many spinning plates in the air. Your goal should be to keep those plates in the air, at least till you can start delegating more. Keeping on top of all those jobs is totally possible if you are organized. If you are the *Free Spirit* sort, you will need to put some self discipline guidelines in place for yourself. I have put organization into three categories:

- Your Office Space

- Your Files

- Your Time

There are a gazillion resources on organizing so this section is not meant to be an exhaustive collection of plans and ideas. People organize in lots of different ways, and what works for one will not work for another. Choose your own style and find out what works for you.

The following is what worked for many of my clients as well as what worked for me and the methods that I have collected from being a chronic organizer myself.

Your Office Space

Whether your office space is in your brick and mortar store, a room in your home, or part of a room in your home, or even in a closet (yep, I've been there, too!), you need to be able to function. Whether you are just starting to design your office, or are currently redesigning, the first step is determining HOW you want your office space to function. Will it be just a place to do your paperwork? A place for staff? Conferences? Meet clients there?

Do you need space for a manager, accountant, or licensing official to have a work space as well as yourself? If you have a home office, do you want it completely secluded from the rest of the house, in a semi-open space so you still can be part of the family or even right out in your family living room? I have a home office in one of my spare bedrooms that doubles as a guest room. My desk and computer table line a wall with my four-drawer locking file cabinet taking up residence in the closet. My floor space is clear so that I can easily convert to a guest room by blowing up a high end, double-high air mattress. My not-too-distant plan is to replace the air mattress with a Murphy bed, which will provide my office with an additional wall cabinet and shelving. Having a laptop offers me the freedom to use my computer anywhere, so I do not have to be chained to my desk when guests are using the room.

Once you decide how you want to use your office space, take a hard look at how it is currently set up. What doesn't belong there? Many offices end up as an unintentional store room. You know, where broken equipment ends up. Items that you were going to return back in 2006 but never did. Items that just belong somewhere else but lost their way and ended up in the corner by your desk. The list of stuff that clogs an office is as unending as the reasons why and how the clutter happens. Look around and get rid of anything that does not belong. Be ruthless! This is YOUR office! Plan and design it your way. If it doesn't fit how you want the office to function, boot it out.

Also look at what isn't working. Is the lighting poor? Too hot or too cold? Not enough work space, file drawers, or shelving? If the paint on the walls had a name, it would be "Dungeon Grey"? Furniture not well placed? Windows don't open without a screwdriver or door won't stay closed without a brick in front of it? Make a list of everything that isn't working, then prioritize and start making everything right.

Choosing your office equipment comes next. We'll start with your desk. The options are endless, but here are a few things to consider.

Price

Obviously, your budget will determine what you get. You can do the college dorm version of concrete blocks with a sheet of plywood on top, to the other extreme of a high end desk purchased from a posh furniture store. There are lots of choices in-between. You can find many good desks in second hand stores. Some will need a little cleaning up, and others will be ready to put into service as soon as you walk out the door. If you go this route, check out all the drawers to make sure they function well. If they do not, is a problem you can easily repair or live with? It is not hard to be dazzled by a cool looking desk, only to find a busted drawer (or two or three) once you get it home.

There are also used office furniture places around as well as salvage stores like the REStore who salvage furnishings from old office, home, and school buildings. Watch for businesses that are remodeling. I have an old tiger oak desk that I purchased from a counseling building that was upgrading their offices, then I refinished it.

Craigslist is another option as well as family and friends who want to rid themselves of a desk they are no longer using. If "pre-owned" is not for you, you can start at places like Office Max or Office Depot. Then move up to the furniture stores like Ikea or one of your local furniture stores. The internet is a great place to search out the really classy high end stores that specialize in office furniture.

Size

Desks come in all shapes and sizes and what you choose is determined on the space you have, the function you determined you want your office to fulfill, and how you normally work. If you don't have a lot of floor space, one idea is to think of options that go up the wall.

A small desk will fit in a small work space but coupled with a hutch top, it will maximize work space and storage. This hutch can be part of the desk, wood cubicles, wire racks, or a board on stacked bricks. As long as the end result gives you adequate work space, this is a good solution to a small space.

Corner desks are also a nice option to utilize your floor space. If you have no idea what is out there, go online and Google office desks. You will see every imaginable size and type.

Function

Office Desk

How do you want your desk to function? Do you want to have a drawer(s) that accommodates hanging files? Do you want to be able to lock your desk? Do you like the wood boards that slide out like a kitchen cutting boards to give you more work surface when you need it? Do you need a large work surface to spread out when you work, or do you function just as well in a small area? Think through on what you will be using your desk for and your personal style of working.

Office Chair

Your office chair is next. Not too much to say here, except to make sure it is comfortable. There will be days that you will be working at your desk for many hours at a time. The most comfortable chairs will adapt to all your movements including sitting upright, reclining, moving from side to side and even slouching. Test drive your chair before you buy. After testing out the good ones, the cheap, uncomfortable ones will make themselves known as soon as you sit down in them.

File Cabinets

File cabinets are the next thing to consider. They are a key item to organizing your office space. A locking file cabinet will be necessary if you have employees, even if your office is in your home. Background checks, fingerprinting, and TB tests are just a few of an employee's file that is required by law to be kept under lock and key.

Due to concerns of identity theft, all client files should be locked up as well. As far as file cabinets go, quality really matters. When I opened my first business, I fell prey to a beautiful 2 drawer oak file cabinet at a big box store that turned out to be a piece of junk. The file drawers only opened 2/3 of the way, which meant I had to blindly dig to the back of the file to get to what I needed. The drawers were constantly falling off the track and I had to brace the file cabinet with one hand to keep it from falling over, even with just one drawer open. The 26 inch deep file cabinets are a better choice, and allow for file growth both in the 2 and 4 drawer versions. My favorite brand is the Hon for stability.

Other items in an office can include a small table for a printer and paper, extra chairs, or a bookcase for reference books and anything else you would like to put on the shelves.

Office Files

No matter what filing system you use, it has to work for you. If your system is too complicated, filing will become a nightmare and you will find it difficult to maintain. If not detailed enough, retrieving information will be nearly impossible.

My Story

When I opened my adult family home, before I even opened my doors, I needed to be inspected by a state licenser to make sure everything was to code. Every possible detail is inspected. They made sure there were no holes in the screens, no dust on the mantel, the hot water was not one degree above 120, and the non-slip strips on the wheelchair ramp was appropriately placed.

The office is also an area of inspection. Since I am often detailed to a fault, my filing system was impeccable complete with color coded files, with each category in alphabetical order. My desk was clear. My licenser was impressed but her hat tip to me came with a warning. She reiterated to me how important it is to be organized and to have a system in place from day one, because as my business grows, my organizational skills will be tested. There will always be more categories and more papers to file.

There are many filing systems out there and there are many resources to help you choose. One resource that helped me when I first started was a book entitled, *Taming the Paper Tiger at Work* by Barbara Hemphill. She gave me ideas on how to overcome filing problems. Because I am such a visual learner, using colored hanging file folders helped me a lot in the beginning. The system I ended up with may not work for you but worked fabulously for me and my system encompassed the following. The Goal: Keep the filing system as simple as you can.

I had three main file drawer categories: 1) Staff, 2) Clients, and 3) Operations.

Staff

Current staff information was filed at the front of the file drawer, each with their own hanging file folder, organized alphabetically. All current staff folders were blue. No particular reason, other than it was my favorite color. I set up an "inactive" file in the back of the file drawer for staff that had left the company.

Initially, I just dropped in a bunch of empty yellow hanging file folders. When an employee left, I just took everything from their blue file and dropped it in a yellow file in the back of the drawer, also transferring their file label, a total process time of about 26 seconds.

There are many reasons to keep old employee files, but good to remember that because of identity theft all employees' files, both new and old, must be locked up. Old employee files must be destroyed after three years. It is actually a felony to keep old employee files past three years.

Most employee files were pretty simply and did not need sub-file folders. Time sheets, training documents, initial application and resume, background checks, discipline and evaluation forms were what most files contained. Setting up separate sub-folders for each of these categories for each employee would have been overkill even for me! If you get too micro-tiny with the filing, you won't maintain it. Pretty soon, you find yourself breaking things down into atoms.

Remember, you file because at some point in the future, you may need to retrieve it. The goal is to be able to know where a document is and be able to retrieve it quickly. I could go to any employee file, new or old, and find the information I needed in about thirty five-seconds. I am not convinced a lesser time would benefit me that much.

I had one file folder in front labeled *Applications*. In this folder I had employment applications, I-9 forms, W-4s and other forms prospective staff would need to fill out. Again, if it was anything about staffing, it went in this drawer.

Clients

Keeping with the same system as my staff files, I maintained color coded files for my clients, using just one color file folders. I maintained an active file in front, and an inactive file in the back of the drawer for clients who had left or passed away.

Because my adult family home ran on the medical model, I maintained a large binder for each client that was broken down into 19 categories. Many of these were required by the state as charting and information updates were required daily. These binders were also required to be accessible by staff. What was in my locked file drawers, were financial agreements and payment statements that were not in the "need to know" category for staff to take care of our residents. If you have clients for whom you do multiple projects, then purchase interior files (manila folders that are shorter than the normal ones), and set up an interior file for each project you have for that client.

Operations

This was by far my largest file, again organized alphabetically using color hanging file folders. Anything that involved running the company was placed here. Categories included:

- Licensing—initial application, current status, receipts

- Inspections—past and current, sub-filed by agency

- Fire Drills—ongoing log

- Venders—each with their own sub-file

- Banking—bank statements sub-filed into years

- Quarterly Taxes—sub-file into years

- IRS—sub-file into years

- State Contracts—(mine was with DSHS)

- Inventory—all

- Budget—on-going

- Business Plan—initial and updates

- Expansion—dreams of where you want to go, business expo, literature, ideas

- Marketing—Sub-filed into modalities like website, market effort, tracking, networking, or event planning

- Community resources—contacts

- Repairs/Improvements—tracking

- Taxes—Business and Occupation taxes (B&O), Employment Security Taxes, Labor & Industry (L&I) all have their sub-file folders here. You can also have just one tax file where you put ALL your tax sub-files, including IRS and quarterly taxes. That way, if you need to retrieve anything having to do with any kind of tax, you will have just one go-to file, where you can pluck out the appropriate sub-file you need.

- Policies and Procedures—how the company is to be run

- Travel—Airline and shuttle bus info to job sites

- Education—upcoming conferences, seminars, classes offered by the local community or technical colleges, and in-house training.

- Masters—one copy of every form I use goes here. I will always have one original to make copies if needed.

- Insurance—Business Insurance policy

Choosing Colors

You can use any color hanging file folders you want. You can stick with one color, or use a different color for each drawer of files, or see how many rainbow colors you can fit into the drawer(s). It's all your choice. Many of these categories won't have any subfolders, and some will have lots. Categories will increase or change according to the business you have. For example, if you use vehicles in your business for delivering supplies or people or getting employees to a job site, you will have a *vehicle* file.

Cross Filing

Here is a word about cross filing: Don't do it! You will drive yourself crazy! On some categories though, it is easy to have more than one category for one element of the business. For instance, if you use vehicles for part of your business, do you file your vehicle insurance sub-file under Insurance or under Vehicles?

It's not a bad idea to set up a copy of your whole filing system, either hard copy or on your computer. Just similar to what I listed above. The name of the main file, and all the sub-files that are in it. If you forget which file that vehicle insurance goes in, just check this cheat sheet. You can tape it to the front or side of the file cabinet for fast easy access. This is especially important if you have someone who helps you file. Just for the record, I would file vehicle insurance in a sub-file under vehicles. If it has anything to do with a vehicle, that's where it goes.

Time to Purge

If you find yourself using a shoehorn to file your papers, it's time to purge. Once a year is usually adequate; but more often if you're having trouble getting those papers in. Try to have at least 1/4 to 1/3 of the file drawer empty so you have room to EASILY file papers as well as room for file growth.

How Long to Save?

How long to save this stuff seems to be a question I get a lot. Here's the scoop from my savvy accountant.

- IRS returns—forever

- Home/business sales or purchases—forever

- Former employees files—three years

- Client Files—forever

- Bank Statements - forever

The IRS now recognizes digital files so I scan in every receipt to my computer.

I purge my files at the beginning of each year, put all the receipts and statements in a plastic bin and date the year. Since I have my receipts saved digitally, it is not really necessary to save my hard copies, but hey, that's just me.

Some of my categories are "running files" like bank statements. After being in business for eight to ten years, that file can get quite fat and take up a quarter of a drawer all by itself. In the cases with old paperwork, I start an inactive file in an empty file drawer, or more often I use a plastic hanging file box from Office Depot. I usually don't need more than two years of bank statements in my current files. I set up my inactive files the same way as the active ones—in alphabetical order.

Your Time

There are a gazillion things that scream for our time. It's not only other people and the urgent situations that seem to constantly pop up, but the voice and confusion in our own heads and our inability to organize our time. I've comprised a list of organizational tips for your time.

I tried to make the list as user friendly as possible. Most of these I have used myself and are basic techniques I recommend to my clients. Some will resonate with you. Others you will quickly disregard. Be willing to give a shot to new ideas, or ideas that you tried before but didn't work well. Try those ideas again by adding a different time, technique, or tweaking it some way. My hope is these tips will help you become less overwhelmed, have decreased stress and be more productive.

Know your highest energy time

Are you a morning person or a night person? When do you power through tasks? Do you have your payroll all done by 10:00 AM or are you just mentally waking up at 1:00 in the afternoon? Develop a morning routine (or afternoon, whichever is your highest energy time).

I am a morning person and it takes me about 45 min. to get myself out of bed and out the door; however, I allow myself an hour and a half. This allows me an additional 45 min. to sit with my coffee, check my calendar, write out a to do list, check email and my business social media sites and even have a short prayer time with my God. It's a time to breathe deeply, relax, have some quiet time and empty my head onto paper, before the craziness of the day begins.

The calendar is for appointments, not a to-do list.

Have only one calendar, two at the most or it will become a nightmare trying to coordinate and maintain them all. I have a 3X5 inch, one-year calendar I keep in my purse, and a calendar in my office. As soon as I make an appointment, I log it on both calendars. At the end of the day, I check both calendars to make sure they match. It's routine now. This keeps me from double booking myself, even when I am out and about.

Many people I know just use the calendars they have on their phones which they have with them wherever they are and this eliminates the need of coordinating calendars. Having a hard copy calendar works for me best while I'm still trying out different calendar apps. Some people use the calendars on their computer, such as Outlook or other calendar programs.

Set goals monthly

Whether these are networking goals, project goals, or improved operations, get them down on paper. You will flounder if you don't know where you are going.

Make lists of supporting tasks for your goals

Your supporting tasks are what will make your goals happen. Break the tasks down into weeks, then days. Every morning, add some of these supporting tasks to your to-do list along with other routine tasks you need to accomplish.

If the list seems daunting, prioritize your tasks. I use the A,B,C method. "A" tasks are *MUST do*; "B" tasks are *would LIKE to do*, and "C" tasks are *would be NICE to do*.

Make it a goal to accomplish at least 5 things from your to-do list every day. What you cannot finish on your to-do list, reschedule in a day timer or on your computer to make sure it will get done.

Develop time frames for your work load

If you don't manage your time, it will manage you. So many times at the end of the day, we wonder where all the hours went. When will you work on your payroll, or inventory, or filing, or marketing, or the specific tasks that will get you closer to your goals?

On Tuesday and Thursday from 2:00-4:00 you could schedule marketing and website tasks.

Wednesday and Friday from 2:00-3:00 could be supporting tasks towards your goals.

Monday through Friday from 8:00-1:00 could be all routine business tasks.

Friday from 3:30-5:00 or 6:00 could be wrap-up time for the week where you file everything in your In-box.

You get the idea. Not every day will go as planned. Some days you will feel like you have just spun your wheels and gotten nowhere. But if you plan times for your work load, those unproductive days will be the exception, rather than the rule.

It's okay to close your door

I loved interacting with my staff. I had an open door policy and most of the time it really was open. But there are times when you REALLY, REALLY have to get stuff done. Sometimes it's not only okay, but necessary, to close that office door. I have had to do this to my own family since my office is now at home. Since I had such a generous open door policy, my staff were always respectful of my time when I told them I was going to close my door for awhile. I checked in with them both before and after I sequestered myself. Not because I had to but to give them time to ask questions or pass on information. I believe it was this courtesy that caused them to be respectful of my time when I needed it. When I needed to close that office door to get stuff done, I half-jokingly told my staff unless there was fire, flood, blood, or death, I did not want to be disturbed. Fortunately, I never heard that knock on the door.

File, file, file

File every day or at least once a week. Try to file at least five documents, or receipts, every day. Write the date at the top of everything you file. At the minimum, file everything in your *To File* box at the end of your work week.

If this job has not been done for awhile, pick a day and time to do the task; or set a timer for one hour and see how much you can accomplish in that hour. Or thirty minutes. Or fifteen minutes.

Develop routines

File routinely. Market routinely. Plan routinely. When you implement routines consistently, this is how habits are formed. Once you have developed good habits of time management, your days will be so much more productive, which decreases your stress.

Delegate where you can

Feelings of being overwhelmed are not uncommon in the world of small business, and yet many owners will not even entertain the idea of delegating. They are so physically, financially, and emotionally submerged in their business, they can't even go there. Some of their reasons are, "It's my baby," or "No one else is trained to do this."

Choose a small task and delegate it to an employee. Be sure to convey specific instructions so it is clear they will do the task to your specifications. Then check in with them in a week or two. This is NOT the same as micromanaging; this is monitoring, which is your job as the owner.

Next, try another task. Go out on a limb here, and mention to your employee that you are open to ideas to make this process or task easier or more efficient. Their ideas just might be better than yours! Delegating can lift a huge weight off your shoulders. Give it a try.

What are you going to say no to?

Owning and running a business takes a tremendous amount of time and energy, especially in the early days. Activities that took up your time pre-business, will need to be thinned out. Some you really liked! Maybe you were active in an organization. Maybe you have taken on projects for others, or taken on volunteer responsibilities, or had a part-time job. Maybe you are into TV a lot, or Facebook, or sports, or—fill in the blank. Take stock of what is really important. You will need to make some hard choices on what you are going to say no to.

What are you going to say yes to?

Now that you have decided what you are going say no to, what are you going to say yes to? What barriers are you ready to blast through? Will you have the courage to say yes to new opportunities, even if they are unfamiliar to you? Will you say yes to trying new ways to think and do? Yes to new ways to spend your time?

Balance your time

Your life as a new business owner will be out of balance for awhile, but that does not mean you should have zilch personal life. Make sure family time is more than just "penciled in." Family is most often where the biggest support comes from. It does not matter if your office is downtown or in a corner of your family room, have a definitive cutoff time for work. When you are at home, truly be at home. If you do not have a family, the advice is the same. Everyone needs down time.

Schedule growth time

Watch for seminars or conferences in your industry. Plan for them. Save for them. Schedule them. Going to these conferences with break out learning sessions are like a shot in the arm when you might feel at your lowest. You will return to work charged with new information and new zest for your business.

Be Disciplined

Being self employed has the illusion of being your own boss. In many ways, you are. You can pull yourself out of bed whenever you feel like it. You can act and dress however you like. You can ship out supplies when it suits you, or be okay with producing a sloppy product or service when you are having a lousy day. No one is there to whip you, nag you or fire you, except maybe your customers, of course.

On the flip side, because you ARE the boss, you have the opportunity to bolt out of bed, dress sharp, and come to work every day with a positive attitude. This is true if your work place is a computer in your home office, or a pizza store six blocks away. You have the opportunity to explore and implement new ideas or tasks, improve on status quo operations, be innovative, or change things that are just not working. How powerful is that?

It does take discipline though, to be this kind of business owner. Your mother is probably not going to coax you out of bed handing you a to-do list that she has made out for you. It really is all about you. In the employment world it's called being a "self starter."

I say being your own boss is an illusion, because in many ways, it is. There will always be others you will be beholding to.

- Your customers

  Without them, you don't have a business.

- Your employees

  Just try to operate any kind of brick and mortar store without them. Treat them poorly, and your business will have a constant staff revolving door, and worse, a circulating reputation of a horrible place to work.

- Federal, state and local licensing agencies

  Most industries have governing rules and regulations you must comply with if you own a business. Most businesses have multiple agencies they must deal with. Restaurants deal with the local health department and city or county regulations dealing with parking restrictions.

  Industries that include licensed professionals such as nurses, nurses aids, beauticians, electricians and contractors, all deal with state agencies, including maintained records of all such licensed staffing. Dry cleaners must comply with waste management regulations. And don't forget all the tax agencies. So even though you have a great deal of power being your own boss, there will always be things you won't have control over.

Be on top of it all

My husband has been one of my best supporters. He often expresses comments about what a good job I do with the business. When I asked him why he thought I was such a good manager, he said it was because I was always on top of everything.

When you are in the thick of things, you usually just charge through the days, weeks, months, and years without really analyzing how you got there, so I asked him to expound on his thoughts. He was unable to be more specific other than to say that I just seemed to get stuff done.

Okay. That is one element of management, but once I really started to think about it, it was a BIG part of it. How do you make sure shifts are covered, supplies arrive when promised, or appointments are kept? How do you know if your customers are happy, or when your payroll will be ready? I have identified two concepts that have helped me stay on top of it all. One is *follow up* and the other is *follow through*.

Follow up

I am very customer service oriented. There seems to be such a lack of customer service these days that I have become conditioned to believe that unless I follow up, a task is not going to get done. I am even going to go out on a limb here, and state that has been my experience, especially when dealing with government agencies. I have not arrived at this opinion arbitrarily. It has been my experience.

There were many times I had to follow up with a task, request, or phone call or bad things would have happened. Sometimes without that follow up, nothing at all would have happened (also a bad thing). There have been numerous venders, staff, customers and agencies that have shown up with their time, their products, phone calls, and appointments as promised in a timely manner. Unfortunately, the ones who don't are becoming the rule rather than the exception. All to say, it becomes your job as business owner to follow up to make sure everything runs smoothly. Here are some examples and tips.

Get detailed information when ordering supplies

Ask and write down the name of the sales representative you are talking to, the date and time of the order, when it will be delivered and who is going to be delivering it (USPS, FedEx, UPS). This habit alone will save you hours of track-down time later, as well as making you look like the detailed, organized person you are.

Writing this down on a piece of scratch paper is not a good idea. It will get lost on your desk. Develop a file folder for every vender. You can purchase order forms online or at such stores like Office Depot or Staples. Post on a calendar when you expect the supplies to arrive. This can be the calendar on your phone or on your office wall or desk, wherever your go-to place is for appointments.

Remember, when a vender says *five-to-ten days* for shipping, that usually does not include weekends and holidays, but clarify that as well. Check off items when they have been delivered.

Follow up if supplies don't come as promised

If supplies don't arrive on the scheduled delivery date, call the very next day and find out why (in your best assertive but kind voice, of course). If you don't call right away, the delay could set you back on your orders. It could also force you to buy the needed product from somewhere else at a more costly price.

There could be very valid reasons for a delay or non-delivery such as snowy road conditions, the delivery went to the wrong place (this has happened to me), or item(s) were out of stock. At least if you know, you can plan accordingly. Don't assume a vender is going to call you right away if the product you ordered is out of stock. You could be waiting for weeks, and not hear anything.

My Story

When I ordered a case of special pads for the residents in my home, I waited a week after their scheduled delivery date before I called. This is way too long.

When I called, I was told there was a mix up in the deliveries and they sincerely apologized. The order would be delivered the following Thursday. When the following Thursday came and went with no delivery, I called again.

This time I was told they had trouble getting my order from THEIR supplier, but they were expecting the order the next day and I would have my supplies by the following Thursday, and "We so apologize".

After the next Thursday came and went with no delivery, I called a third time in the morning and received yet another "reason" why I did not have my shipment.

> This time, I presented an ultimatum. I either wanted a phone call from my sales rep, or my delivery by 4:00 PM the next day, or they were to cancel my order and I would change venders. They didn't, so I did.

Set boundaries and keep your cool

You probably can imagine how frustrating this whole process was. I had to scramble to find a local substitute product that would work, which cost me time and money. What angered me most was no call backs and what seemed to be an endless stream of excuses with no attempt to keep me informed, much less keep me as a customer.

There WILL be delivery delays. When talking to venders, it's important to remember to be respectful with these challenging follow up calls. What is REALLY going through you head is something like this:

"What is wrong with you? Are you a moron? Do you need me to come down there and do your job for you?"

Being respectful is part of being professional, regardless of the ineptness of others. Set boundaries and be willing to walk away if you are consistently receiving poor service. There are always options.

By the way, this works in your personal life as well. Please allow me to indulge in a personal story of my own.

My Story

When I was having reception issues with my satellite company, the online tech support was not helpful. It was deemed that I needed a field technician to come out to my property to troubleshoot the problem.

I scheduled an appointment three days out with their usual window time of "between 8:00 AM and noon."

That day and time came and went with nary a technician in site. By 12:30, I was on the phone to see what was up. The satellite company did not even have me on their calendar that day. Come to find out, the person who scheduled my appointment time neglected to pass that on to the Field Technician Department.

"We so apologize. Can I set up another appointment for you?"

I know even the best run companies will occasionally drop a ball so I said *sure*. I was getting a little nervous here as I needed to leave for an out-of-state job in a few days and wanted a working system for my family for the six weeks I would be gone.

Again, I set up another appointment time three days out (my last days at home). This time the window of time was between noon and 4:00. That day and time also went by without seeing a technician, so by 4:15 I was on the phone with the company.

This time, I was told the field technician for my area "called in" (no explanation for what that means).

"We so apologize, can I make another appointment for you?"

After two no-shows from them, I politely (through clenched teeth) said no. Because of the of two previous appointments in which they had dropped the ball, I needed to see a technician at my place before the end of day or they could come remove all their equipment and I would transfer my service to a company who valued me as a customer.

After some checking, the woman on the phone came back on the line and said there would be a technician at my home by 6:15. And indeed there was.

He was the most kind, apologetic person ever! He discovered that a cable line was wired wrong by the first technician who set my service up. This long scenario is to make two points. 1) Following up is important in order to get what you want, and 2) be willing to walk away from a service that consistently provides poor service.

My ultimatum to the satellite company was not an idle threat. It would have been a hassle to change my TV service provider, but I consider that minor compared to years of constant frustration of dealing with any company who does not give a rip about their customers.

Follow up with your staff

If there are classes your employees are required to take in order to do their jobs, make sure that is documented in their files. My staff was required to have CPR and first aid, Food Handler's Permit, yearly state caregiver licensing, and continuing education classes, each having various expiration dates. Some were every two years, some every three years, and some every year.

The above listed classes were the responsibility of the employee, but my job to make sure it was documented in their file. I don't really know anyone who just loves to spend four hours taking a CPR class, but a state licenser who drops buy to inspect your files really doesn't care that your employee has not had the time or the money to take the class. You will be the one to take the heat as the owner.

I have had to draw a hard line on this, but only after a time or two of receiving citations due to being too soft on my employees. I made out a spread sheet every year with employees listed on the side of the sheet, and required paperwork across the top. Then I filled in the dates of when each expiration date was for each required document for each employee.

I gave a one month reminder to employees when they had to renew a class or document. If I did not receive any response, at two weeks, they received a warning that they would be unemployed on the expiration date of the needed document. This was hard because many of my best staff were hard working and responsible workers (except in this one area) that I would hate to lose, but I had reached a point where I was no longer willing to take the heat for others.

Schedule changes and shift trades are also something to follow up on. I allowed staff to arrange their own trades but had to be signed off by me before they were considered to be a done deal. A Shift Trade log book was initiated with the two staff listed, the dates and shift times that were to be affected and a line for my signature. This needs to be reviewed frequently as you always want to know who is coming in to work and when. No surprises.

Follow up on work performance as well. Monitor what is and is not working well. Monitor WHO is not working well. If you are working with a staff member to strengthen their skills or performance, have an open line of regular communication on how they are doing.

Follow up with appointments

When you make an appointment with someone, or they make an appointment with you, call the day before or at the very least, several hours before, to confirm. People get busy and forget, or they overbook themselves. A simple call beforehand can eliminate a whole bunch of frustration from a no-show appointment.

Follow Through

While following up is all about correcting, or avoiding the mistakes and deficiencies of others, following through is all about *your* actions. Following through has a twofold benefit.

Not only does it prevent disastrous situations from happening, it demonstrates you are a person of your word.

Have you promised a particular staff member a raise "soon" (code word for I don't know when)? Announced there will be a staff Christmas party this year; then there wasn't? Told customers you will have a new product or service out this spring, but nothing shows up? It does not take long before people no longer take you seriously.

I have five children, ten grandchildren and have had more employees than I can count, so I have developed a heightened B.S. meter. I can tell within minutes when someone is trying to skirt an issue by shoveling up a load of B.S. I would be foolish to think I am (or you are) the only one who could detect someone trying to skirt an issue. Your customers and staff will know when you are being disingenuous, especially if this becomes a habit.

If a staff member confronts you on a task you promised to carry out but have not done so, be honest with them about it. Don't brush them off. Give them an honest answer. Watch your words. Don't promise what you don't know you can deliver. And when you can't deliver, be honest about the reasons why.

So why don't we follow through? If you know where some of the ruts are in the road, you can avoid them. I have listed a few places where you can get stuck, and how to get your "tires" out of that rut so you can complete that promise, or task.

Not Enough Time

Small business owners wear a myriad of hats and sometimes there really isn't time to do everything. If you promised someone that you would do a task, then that task becomes your priority if you value your reputation as being a person of your word. Everything seems to come down to prioritizing. And that starts at the beginning of your day with your to-do list. Review the section *Be Organized* in Chapter 4.

Note if you are consistently assigning certain tasks in the "C- would be nice to get done" category, when they really should be assigned an "A" or "B" status. Look for the time-wasters in your day, including distractions. Everyone gets the same amount of hours a day. Often, we don't need more hours, we just need to utilize the ones we have more efficiently.

Not Enough Money

Entrepreneurs generally fall into two different kinds of thinkers: 1) The idea people (also called visionaries), and 2) the detail people. You are blessed if you are a combination of both, or your business is a partnership with one of each kind of thinking. Most of us fall heavily into one category or the other.

The idea people are great! They can actually see where their business is going to be ten years down the road with such clarity and excitement that you fully expect to see it all transpire tomorrow. The problem is, they don't know how to get there.

It takes time, planning, and money, and sometimes the money never comes. Loans fall through, the economy makes a downturn, expenses and overhead are too high, or the customer base you counted on just was not there. Too many of these elements hit at one time or for sustained lengths of time, and discouragement sets in. You end up in a rut.

The detail person is also great! They know how to massage, tweak, or even squeeze a budget if necessary. They come up with new marketing ideas, shake up staffing needs, or implement new ways to sell their products or services. The problem with a detail person is they often get so focused on the details, they lose site of the big picture of where they are going.

You CAN be both a visionary and a detail entrepreneur. It takes some practice, but you can reap the benefits of both strengths. How does this all relate to money you might ask? Determine where you want your business to go. Be that visionary. Then set those details in motion to get you there. Find the resources you will need. Prioritize the budget. Be creative with your marketing and overhead. But don't let the lack of money paralyze you. Find ways to make your goals work.

Fear

Fear can be debilitating. So what is there to fear? Virtually anything and everything! Fear of making a wrong decision; or none at all. Fear of not being liked, or saying the wrong thing, or making a decision at the wrong time. Fear of what the future may hold, the economy, global warming or the Godzilla's hiding in the ocean.

As you can see, fear can grow from a small uncertainty, to a massive unrealistic monstrous fear that can cripple you to the point of a complete standstill.

Personally, I think we give too much weight to fear. So what if you have to confront that new employee about their rude responses to customers? Chances are, they may not realize how that affects your bottom line, or they just need to learn different ways to respond. Will they hate you? I doubt it. Can it turn into a great learning experience? Probably.

Here is a big one. You get a letter from the IRS, and you know you are late filing your taxes. Do you file it in a drawer, unopened, or do you slice that envelope open and read what they have to say?

My accountant tells me many of the clients she takes on with tax issues, bring in stacks of unopened letters from the IRS and other state tax agencies. Fear can absolutely cripple a person.

So how do you approach such crippling fear? Just notice it. Notice the emotion, then move right along to action. Do your pros and cons list on difficult decisions and listen to your gut instinct. If you have a problem employee, customer, or vender, but hate confrontation (usually for fear of not being liked), think in terms of what the alternative is.

If the offending person is an employee, and you do not follow up, your business will be negatively affected in many ways. Lost customers, and discord among other staff to name a few. I probably don't have to tell you the consequences of not following through with the IRS. When I have a decision to make, I ask myself what is the best choice for my business.

Lack of Know-How

I know a gentleman who will charge ahead with any task. He will tackle anything. The problem arises when he gets in the middle of a project and gets stumped on a certain aspect before completion. This lack of knowledge to solve the problem causes the project to come to a screeching halt that can last weeks, months, or even years.

There is nothing shameful about admitting you don't know everything. Good planning ahead of time helps, but sometimes situations pop up that you had no way of anticipating. There are ways around this. For one thing, you can look up a solution to a problem on the internet. You can find out how to do virtually ANYTHING on the internet.

Once I typed in how to fillet a whole salmon, and I had a choice of four YouTube videos to watch. Help can be found on the internet for networking, business expansion, staffing issues, product or service marketing, or any other problem-solving issues you might have. Just type in "how to_____" and fill in the blank.

Ask friends, family, or colleagues if they could help you with your project by sharing their ideas, or by helping you brainstorm.

Research the project at the library or buy a book or two covering the information you want to know. (Amazon is my go-to place for books and I almost always choose the used book version over the pricy brand new book).

Contact your local professional organization in your area to see if they can help, or can point you in the direction of someone who can. If you are attempting something like a simple physical expansion or remodel of your brick and mortar store, check out the local specialty store you need.

The big jobs, like electrical and plumbing, are best left to the professionals but even in those areas, there are aspects that even I can do. My town has a local, privately-owned hardware store that is THE place to go. It seems every town has one of these. If you go in and ask them for a widget part for a 1952 obscure piece of equipment, they either have it or can order it and the widget will be here by Tuesday. Every sales rep in the store can talk you through any problem you have. A great resource place.

And lastly, hire a consultant if needed. Sometimes an expert's advice is worth its weight in gold, or your business hide.

My Story

I had a problem with an employee. She took off way too many days, lied about her reasons for needing them, could not seem to finish a shift without phoning the manager for help, ticked off her fellow coworkers and my clients, and refused to follow safety procedures.

This employee worked for me way too long, because I had not yet learned how to put on my big girl pants. The inevitable happened when she got hurt by not following safety procedures, then went out on an industrial claim. I did not want this employee back but it is very dicey to try to terminate an employee who is out on an injury claim. Actually it is illegal, regardless of how it happened.

I had just recently attended a class on terminating employees at my local community college presented by a consulting firm. They were the first ones I turned to for help with this delicate process. They were invaluable in helping me with other aspects such as revamping my job description and imparting more tips on protecting myself and my business. When hitting the wall of needing to terminate someone, but lacking the know-how to do it in a way to protect myself, hiring a consulting firm was the best decision I could have made.

There are many ways to progress past the knowledge barrier, as you can see. Just focus on the ways to get it done rather than the part that is stumping you and keeping you at a complete standstill.

I Just Don't Want To Do That

Sometimes we have a little four-year-old child running around inside of us throwing a temper tantrum. At some point, we all have to be an adult and just "buck up." There are ways to blast through unpleasant or tedious tasks. If you detest filing, set a kitchen timer for an hour or even fifteen minutes if that is all you think you can handle.

Do the tedious tasks during your highest energy time of the day; make sure they aren't constantly relegated to the bottom of your to-do list. Set a time frame for yourself—such as from 10:00-11:00 will be your time to return phone calls. Approach your work schedule like you are working for, and collecting a paycheck from, someone else. Would you hire you?

If you really notice that you are dragging your feet on jobs that need to be done, assess why. It could be any number of the above reasons. Sometimes you even have to set rules for yourself like "I will not allow myself a second cup of coffee until I finish these phone calls, or this job description draft, or _____." You fill in the blank. Then reward yourself with a break, a cup of coffee or tea, or anything you want. For me, it's a bit of chocolate.

And last, foot dragging can progress to a complete stand-still or the collapse of an important aspect of your business. If all else fails, delegate. If doing payroll is just not your thing and causing your stomach to tie in knots every payroll period, then by all means, farm it out. Hiring an assistant to help lighten your load and ensure tasks are done in a timely manner will be like a breath of fresh air.

CHAPTER 5

The Four Management Styles that Will Kill Your Business

Don't Be this Guy

Your management style affects your relationship with your employees, but is also directly or indirectly responsible for as much as 30% of your bottom line. Poor management is one of the larger causes for the staff revolving door. It's been said that people don't leave bad companies, they leave bad bosses. This has certainly been true in my past.

Listed below are the three most well-known problem bosses. You may recognize some of these management types from your own working past. Remember how you felt working for such a boss.

The Micromanager

I think everyone has worked for one of these bosses at some point in their lives. Micromanagers often don't trust anyone with any aspect of their business. They often are a perfectionist and even if they do assign you a task they are never happy with the results.

They relish the details, and want to guide you through every aspect of the process. They may try to fool you by letting you think you are responsible for accomplishing a task but have difficulty letting go. As soon as there is a detail that does not meet their specifications, they swoop down with sharp criticism. "Don't sweat the small stuff," is not in their vocabulary.

Excessive attention to the "micro" due to lack of trust is at the core of the micromanager. They fear getting in trouble by their "higher ups" if mistakes are made, so they must avoid any mistake at any cost. Being able to distinguish between the details and the big picture is difficult for them and often the micromanager is not even aware he is micromanaging.

The destructive part of this style is the demoralizing effects it has on staffing. Who wants to work at a job where you are not trusted to do your job, you never know what to expect, and doing your best will never be good enough? Working in the micromanager's absence brings everything to a standstill because employees are fearful to make even the smallest decision, knowing it will probably be wrong by the micromanager's standards.

The solution is to learn to relax a little. If your employees have been trained well, you should have every confidence in their ability to accomplish the tasks and projects you have set out for them to do. If delegating is hard for you, start with just one employee to delegate to. Be very clear about the outcome you want. Rather than TELLING them about how to do the job, ASK them if they have any questions about the how-to of the job.

They may ask you, and you can share your preferred methods, then let them choose. Let staff know you will be checking in with them at various milestones in the project. Convey your openness to assist with guidance if they have problems or get stuck along the way, again, letting them be the initiator of problem solving.

More guidance may be needed for less-experienced employees. Be more involved for critical projects, or brand new ones that even you are less familiar with. When mistakes are made, or a project is not moving along as fast or as well as needed, resist the urge to jump in and fix it.

Collaborate with the person in charge. Find out what isn't working or what caused the error, then brainstorm a plan to rectify it. It is up to the employee you assigned the task, to fix it, not you. Employees become empowered when they know you not only trust them with the task, but also trust them to have the ability to problem solve when things go wrong. And, when you don't bring your whip to every check-in meeting, they become bold with their problem solving solutions.

The Manager Who Lacks Backbone

Managers at their best are leaders. In this case, a *spineless leader* is an oxymoron. These managers are often people pleasers. Their conflict solving style is usually avoidance. It takes them forever to put out the business fires that crop up every day, or they let them grow so big it threatens their business. They keep the horrible employee way too long, and let venders and customers define the boundaries of their business.

Speaking of boundaries, they don't have any, so employees never know where THEIR boundaries are. They are often disorganized, and the fear of conflict seems to drive their operational style. They are obsessed with fairness, but at the same time, will throw team members under the bus to save face with the higher ups if projects have not gone well. Sometimes, their lack of ability has nothing to do with fear of not being liked, but is actually perfectionism. This "disease" can be fatal to a company as the fear of making a wrong decision, paralyses them from making any decision.

Being a business owner is definitely not for the faint of heart. It takes courage to make appropriate decisions. While being fair is an admirable goal, it is unrealistic to make life fair for everyone. Life itself is not always fair. Nor will you make everyone happy. Conflict will happen. There will be differences of opinion. Not everyone will like you or the decisions you make. What's so bad about that?

Will your reputation be ruined if you don't cave to an employee's request? Will you turn into a pumpkin if you define workplace boundaries and hold people accountable to them? Again, when making decisions or confronting behavior that is not acceptable, keep the health of your business the focus of your conversation.

The Manager with the Big Head

While the previous manager lacks backbone, the manager with the big head has the opposite problem. He's the guy (or gal) who is so self-absorbed that he pays little attention to his staff. He'll walk right by them in the morning without so much as a hello.

These managers are not very good listeners. Staff requests are blown off and customer service is not taken seriously. They might appear to be a slacker, but in reality, just feel they are too important to do anything that does not fit their time frame. They have a sense of entitlement, and will ask others to do their personal work, and will take credit for the ideas and work of their staff. They will be out on the golf course, or out in their boat, while their staff are awaiting the needed supplies they were promised two weeks ago.

Most business owners or managers won't last long operating in this manner. Staff will leave and customers simply won't return. Being appreciated, according to many studies, is the number one factor that helps keep employees engaged with their work. A business owner who believes the world revolves around him is sure to be on track for a failing business. It is wonderful to get out of your own head now and then, and smile at your staff. Ask them how their morning is going. Ask them if they have everything they need for the day. Be generous with praise when it has been well earned. Truly listen when your customers or staff have issues they want to discuss, then deeply examine what actions you could take to make their experience better.

The Manager with No Integrity

Everyone has at least heard of this guy. He's the one who will offer to pay employees under the table, or will refuse to pay overtime when it is worked. He will definitely throw his employees under the bus when confronted by his own supervisor, or faced with a customer problem.

Like the manager with the big head, his word means little. He rarely follows through with promises such as promotions or pay raises, and may even terminate an employee and never give them their last paycheck.

They operate on the very edge of legal and will even put their employees in dangerous positions by asking them to falsify (or "fudge") reports. These managers don't necessarily have to step over the legal line, they can just operate from an unethical standpoint.

A business needs to make money but to make money off the backs of customers through shady dealings, or shoddy merchandise or services, will surely come back to bite that owner.

Business owners must walk their talk which builds trust among staff and the public. New federal guidelines are coming into place to protect the public, putting business owners at risk for corporate and personal prosecution for unethical practices. The amounts of fines are often determined by how much or how little effort the business has made to set up ethical guidelines to prevent misconduct in the first place.

A variety of reasons, including the financial squeeze of a poor economy can push an owner to make decisions, or even look the other way, from conduct that would be deemed unethical. An ethical approach to business combines a deep concern and respect for the law, your customers and your staff. It all begins with you, the business owner.

CHAPTER 6

Keeping the Passion

You love what you do. You love your products and services. You have a piece of the American dream. You are the owner of your own business! But there will come a day when you reflect on those long fourteen-hour days you need to keep things running smoothly.

The daily grind of being a business owner can be very tiring, both mentally as well as physically. It's easy to get so caught up in the daily never-ending to-do lists that you tend to forget your vision of where you want your business to go. Your initial excitement fades as you focus on just getting through each day. You might start asking yourself, "What have I gotten myself into?"

Self-doubt is normal but there are a few tricks to remind yourself how wonderful it really is to own your own business.

The Vision Board

The law of attraction is based on "like attracts like." Positive thoughts will attract positive results, while negative thoughts will attract negative results. James Redfield puts it another way: "Where attention goes, energy flows." This may be a little *woo-woo* for some of you like it is for me.

The rigorous scientific testing for the law of attraction seems to be missing, along with a little too much subjective data that is hard to measure. Nevertheless, I believe there is something to this, even if it is still considered pseudoscience by many. I believe our self talk does have a huge impact on our actions (or lack of).

I believe our memories can be short and our dreams can get lost as we take on the business of life—or a new business. The vision board is based on the law of attraction, but there is nothing magical about a vision board. It is simply a tool to inspire you, keep you on track, and remind you where you are going and why.

It helps you clarify your dreams and goals and gives you a visual of what your better life looks like. Some people will spend an entire day, or even a weekend, putting their vision board together. I put mine together in a couple of hours. Here is the jest of a vision board.

A corkboard of any size works best. Mine is 3ft x 4ft. I found mine at a yard sale, but you can find them at thrift stores or buy them new at any office supply store.

In the center, put whatever is important to you. I have a small needlepoint scripture verse in the center of my board that says, "I can do all things through Christ who strengthens me."

This is my reminder of where I get my strength when my days are hard. Some people put a picture of themselves in the center as a reminder of what they feel confident they can accomplish. Others will put a picture of their family in the center as a reminder of why they are on the journey they are on.

Maybe your goal is a specific car, or a trip, or new home. This is where magazines come into play. Cut out pictures of the things you don't have snapshots of.

Putting this in the center of the board is only a suggestion. You can stick it in a corner and have everything else radiate out like sun rays. Creativity is the name of the game here.

Next, you can put anything else on your board you like. If you love to golf and have a goal of spending more time on the golf course (or owning one), stick a tee into your board or a magazine picture of a golf course.

If you are very girly, line your board with ribbons or tack material up and tie it back to resemble frilly curtains. Stick up pictures of books, or someone doing a book signing, if you are trying to write one. If you plan to go global with your product, pin up a small map or pictures of Italy or the country you want to venture to first.

Your vision board will probably not be static. It will evolve and constantly change as you take down accomplished goals and put up new ones. Your interests will change as well.

I love to learn and reap huge chunks of information through seminars and conferences. Unfortunately, the really good ones run several thousand dollars and are only offered one time a year. I narrow down my selection to one, then put their brochure up on my vision board as my big yearly educational goal. About a third of the board is dedicated to inspirational quotes. These come from everywhere. When I hear one that really resonates with me, I'll type it out, print it off, then cut it out with my fancy decorative scissors and pin it up on my board. Here is a sampling of what inspires me and keeps me going.

- Believe what you cannot see

- Finish what you started

- Think of ways I can, instead of excuses why I can't

- Successful people will do the hard things that others won't

- A single action is worth a thousand words

- Knowledge is not enough. Only action produces results

- I am not afraid of tomorrow because I know God is already there

- The biggest challenge is in your head. Once you overcome that, you can go on auto pilot

- God is greater than any problem I have.

- You cannot discover new oceans unless you have the courage to lose sight of the shore.

Here are two more tips regarding a vision board. The first is to put it somewhere very visible. Either over your desk or beside your desk in your office would be an excellent place. Its effectiveness will be exceedingly diminished if it ends up behind a door or in a closet. The second tip is to remember the vision board has no special powers. It cannot start a website or contact customers. What it can do is inspire and motivate you when you feel you have lost your way. View it often—as I do mine—and it will help you remember why you are on this journey.

Are You Still Teachable?

One of the qualifying criteria an employer will want to know about a prospective employee is how teachable they are. Are you still teachable? There are many reasons why someone would not be teachable. They could have been in the industry for a long time and feel like they already know everything there is to know. They could be very young and immature, resent being told what to do or have a chip on their shoulder. They could have a strong, independent personality, thinking they can do things on their own without help. Or it's the opposite, being very timid and afraid to ask for help.

There was a commercial on TV many years ago from a university of which I can no longer remember, but I do recall their ending proclamation. "If someone you know, knows more than you, about the subject that you know best, you have some catching up to do."

Read that statement again. As a business owner, you probably know your product or service backward and forward. But really, do you know absolutely everything? Have you been in the industry so long that you absolutely cannot learn a single thing more? Let me tell you, there are always new things to learn. The best business owners will embrace a love of learning to ensure they remain on the cutting edge of their industry. Technology is moving so fast, there will always be new products, services, processes and systems coming down the pike.

Learn and Tell

Be excited about learning new things. Go to conferences and seminars. Read books and subscribe to industry publications. Join industry-related professional groups or Meet-ups. Listen to webinars and podcasts. You may think you have no time in your busy schedule to fit in one more thing, but really, this stuff is important enough to carve out a portion of your week, and your budget, and dedicate it to education.

A good many industries are advancing at warp speeds and if you don't stay on top of advancements you will be left behind. And this is not just about advancements of your particular product or service. It's also new advancements in marketing, customer service, business practices, laws and regulations, employee issues, and a host of other subjects that you would benefit from.

During the years I owned my tea room, I went to the yearly tea convention in Las Vegas (Don't start; I've already heard all the jokes!). I learned about estate teas, how to conduct tea tastings, the art of mixing flavored teas, packaging your own private label teas, then marketing them. I learned about tea and food pairings, new tea room recipes and marketing strategies. One year, I even took my manager with me. We came back pumped and couldn't wait to try out our new ideas.

Now it's time to tell. Tell your staff. Have a training day or at the very least, a staff meeting dedicated to just sharing all the cool stuff you just learned.

Print out a synopsis of the seminars you attended, discuss them, then get feedback from your staff. Your goal is to get them as excited as you are. A once-a-year convention is probably not enough to keep your staff (or you) excited through an entire year.

Plan on having an industry update as an agenda item every few months at your staff meeting. Share what you just learned from an article you read, or the book you just finished. Many managers hold back on the pass-down of information to employees. Information is power, and he who holds all the power, remains the boss. Somehow, managers think if employees know the same stuff they do, this will somehow diminish the management position. Maybe managers don't think their staff members are interested. If a staff member is there just to collect a paycheck, the manager may be right. But do you really want that type of employee working for you anyway?

My Story

I visited a tea shop in my local mall after I had closed my own tea room. This was not a food establishment like mine was, just a place to buy bulk and prepackaged teas. I asked the sales clerk about several different teas and his response was "I don't know" to all of my questions.

I recognized one tea that I loved and often purchased from Canada. When I asked the clerk if the tea came from Canada, he said, "All of our teas come from America," which of course, they do not. I was not asking where the distributors were, I was asking where the tea came from.

Just to confirm this sales associate really was ignorant on tea, I asked him how to make a great cup of tea. My fears were confirmed. It was evident this employee was filling a plug-the-hole need by the store proprietor. I bought my favorite tea, and never returned. Sad.

Tell your customers. Some customers will not be interested. They are very busy and are in and out of your establishment in a blink of an eye. They are not interested in any expanded knowledge you have to impart. They know what they want and often are under time deadlines to get it.

Their body language gives them away. They rapidly shift their weight from side to side, fidget, glance down at their watch eight times within the five minutes they are in your store and cut every one of your sentences off.

If you are bursting at the seams with excitement and are compelled to pass on new information to these time-constricted customers, stick to a six-ten word sentence, max. They won't hear anything you have to say after that.

But then there are customers who want to know everything about your product or service, not just the cost. They will ask you about your processes, how long you have been in business, why your product or service is better (know your competition!), how they can best use your product or service, what are the advantages, are there better products coming out, where you plan to distribute to next, or just the history of your product or service and how it has evolved over the years.

As an example there are a gazillion flower shops out there. Why would a customer choose yours over another? Many of today's customers are not just looking for bargain basement prices. They are looking for a connection, a business relationship, a product or service they can trust, a business owner who is so passionate about his products or service, it almost screams out: *I care enough about my customers to give them the best.*

It all starts with you, the owner.

Keep Rowing the Boat

As I mentioned above, running your own business is hard work. Keep in mind, everyone is watching you—your employees, your customers, and your community. You set the tone for the workplace environment. Be excited! Come to work every day with a spring in your step. Tackle the day's tasks with enthusiasm. Be fired up about learning and trying new ways to advance your business. If you stop rowing the boat, don't be surprised if your staff stops rowing as well. Keep on rowing. You'll get through the hard stuff. The seas will smooth out. After all, you ARE the exceptional business owner.

About the Author

Arlene Doeden's early work experience was in the medical field as Nurse and EMT/Paramedic, working with private ambulance companies. She was also privileged to work as a volunteer firefighter for nine years, advancing to Senior Medical Captain. Teaching CPR, First Aid and EMT skills both in the classroom and back lots of oil refineries, showcased Arlene's ability to help others function during stressful and difficult situations.

Taking a break from the medical world in 2002, she was smitten by the entrepreneur bug and opened a tea room. In 2005, she opened two Adult Family Homes.

Arlene now works as an Executive Coach for small businesses as well as a Home Organization Coach. Her vast experience working in administrative roles with patients, clients, and coworkers, brings out Arlene's natural ability to teach and mentor.

Arlene has received her coaching education from Mentor Coach LLC, an International Coaching Federation (ICF) accredited school.

She can be reached at
ArleneDoedenExecutiveCoaching.com